A Celebration of Birth

By Sheila Kitzinger

Copyright © 1986 by Sheila Kitzinger

Text and front cover photographs by Eleanor Enkin; back cover photograph by Polly Kitzinger.

First printing, 1986, in the United States of America.

All rights reserved. No part of this book may be reproduced or transmitted in any form or by any means, except as is expressly permitted by the 1976 Copyright Act or in writing from the author or her agent, who may be contacted through Pennypress, Inc., 1100 23rd Avenue East, Seattle, Washington 98112.

Library of Congress Number 86-062953
ISBN 0-937604-08-9

Introduction

In these batik paintings I have tried to express the awareness of inner life which many women feel when they are pregnant, and something of the intensity of sensation in childbirth. The accompanying words are not intended to be descriptive, but reflect my own feelings as I did each painting. They were done with a mixture of candle and beeswax on cotton, using brushes and a tjanting, a Javanese style wax pen through which the melted wax streams in a thin line.

The themes include some of the mixed emotions that a woman may have during pregnancy, the sense of the fetus as an intruder who has taken over her body, as well as the delight of knowing that a new life is growing inside her. The rhythms of birth are often painful and call on all our courage, strength and capacity for endurance. But they are also exciting, like great ocean waves rolling onto the shore and breaking with a roar, then receding to build up once more and come rolling in again.

About the Birth Symbol on the Back Cover

My explorations in batik started when I worked, together with my daughter Polly, on a long and lavish scarf depicting birth symbols from other cultures. A symbol from the scarf is illustrated on the back cover.

Throughout history, and even in pre-history, in many different cultures the concept of the life-giving vagina has been an important symbolic motif in women's weaving and other crafts. Men have usually not known what it meant.

The birth symbol takes the form of a hooked diamond, sometimes with a cross representing the fetus inside of the diamond. There are 17 structurally distinct variations on this basic theme which appear in artifacts made by women in cultures all over the world. They can often be discovered, for example, in traditional rugs and wall-hangings woven by women.

The sign represents both vagina and uterus and is the counterpart of the male phallic symbol. Whereas everyone is aware of phallic symbolism in art, the birth symbol has been largely ignored. Throughout the Middle East and North Africa, large parts of Asia and South America, and in the Western Pacific, this strong cultural code has been largely invisible because we have looked at designs with men's eyes and have interpreted visual symbols with man-made language.

The birth symbol represents the power which is released from deep within a woman's body, on the high flood of which a baby is brought to life.

Sheila Kitzinger

Conception

Books taught us that the ovum is a passive blob of matter
waiting patiently
for the onslaught of spermatozoa.
Like a pale moon
helpless and inert
she is invaded
by those miniscule and reckless Argonauts
voyaging from testicles to crescent Fallopian tubes.

The authors, male, have got it wrong.

The ripe ovum dances
in hormonal rhythm
with seasons of desire and estrual tides.
She is woman's inner sun
light-charged, shimmering
and like a powerful magnet
draws multitudes toward her energy.

Beginnings

Small as a hazelnut
the embryo tucks itself into the capsule of her uterus
unguessed at and unknown.
Fruit of love or lust
of partnership or exploitation
the seed uncurls
like a sprouting bean
or pocket sea-horse
head top-heavy, budding limbs, ridged back, pointed tail
tissues frail as a butterfly's wings
and light as an egg-shell.

In the cradle of the pelvis

Drawing nourishment from lace-fronds of its life-giving tree
the fetus child unfurls
little Buddha, marine creature, a floating astronaut
yet rooted in me
hidden doll in the toy-box
child to be.

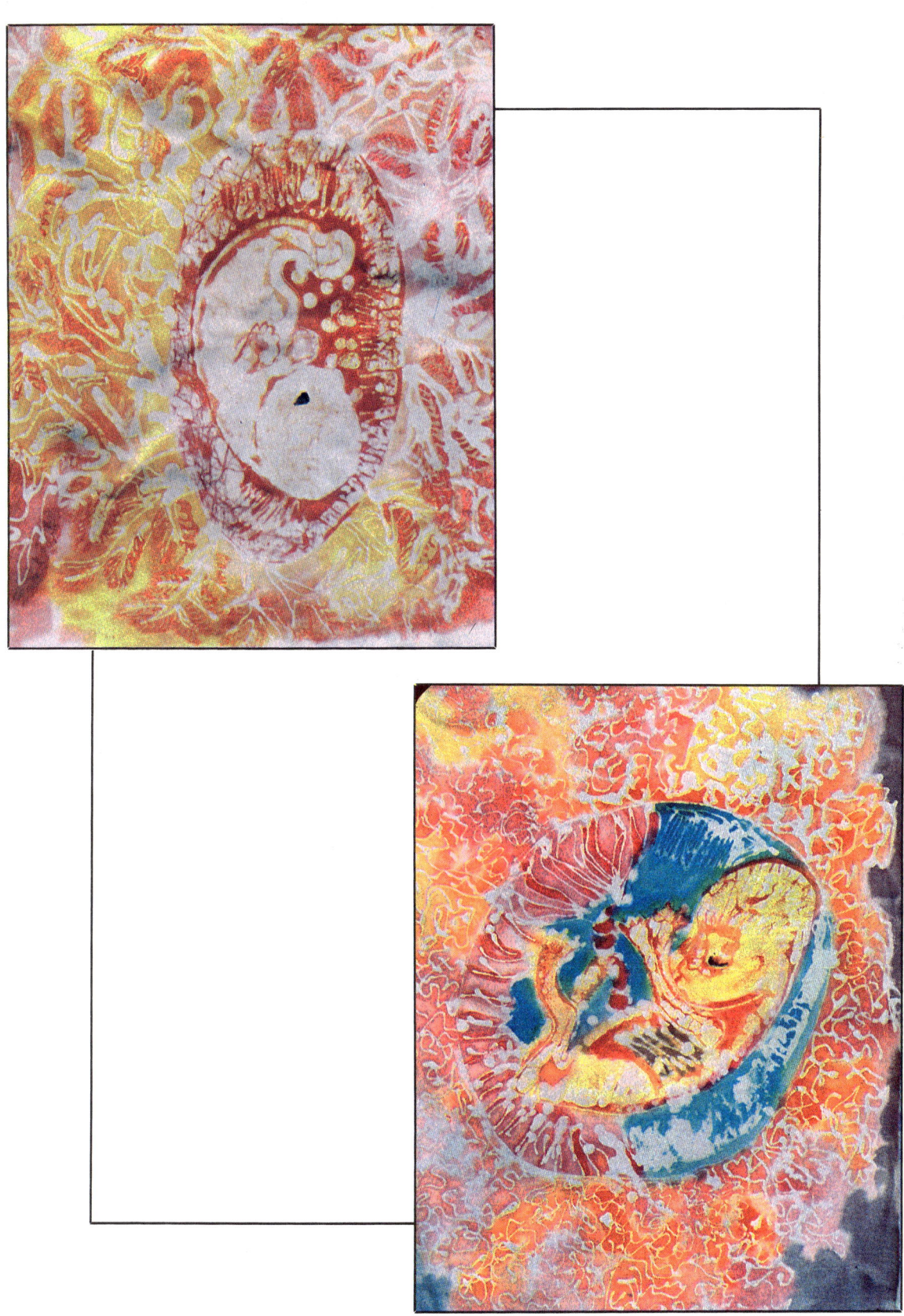

The invader

A stranger uninvited
brute interloper
wallowing in its intra-uterine sea.
The woman who did not plan or want it so confronts herself
and her desires and fears
and who she is and what she means to be.

All over the world
women have sharpened knives, drunk poison and still
this arrogant, pulsing life has clung tenaciously
in the cherishing nest of the womb.
The weeping in the night, the terror, degradation
the desperate longing to escape
have not shaken this fruit from the branch.

With child

A woman with child, melon-ripe, peach-firm.
Blood, grape-red, rushes in her veins
swirls in the cavern of her pelvis
pours through placenta and pulsing cord.
She sees, hears, smells, touches more keenly
with animal vitality.
She is a ship sailing on a swelling sea
toward a sure harbor.

Flower fetus

A flower glows fuchsia-red in the darkness
grows plump cell on cell
firm flesh, soft down, ripening
in its own time.
In the depths of the flower fetus is a jeweled heart.
It beats with the sound of galloping horses
as they speed, white manes flying
across empty spaces
in this small, locked house of the womb.

Bearing this flower in me
I am one with all life.

The breaking of the waters

The giant wave rises to a peak
breath-stopping
and the world splits open.

Waters flow
and on their salt flood a child
presses deep, stinging sweet
and urgent for birth.

Birth passion

I am the tree of life
root, branch and flower.
Energy flows from the center of the earth
the power of all creation.

I share the birth of every growing thing
and my opening
and each passionate urge
is a shout of joy.

The crowning

Primeval energy fixes her to earth
like an oak tree rooted deep.
Rush upon rush pours through her body.
"I am not pushing, I am being pushed."
The pod swells, skin prickles, vagina burns.
"It is not possible!"

Gently now, here comes the head.

"I can't ... I can't ...
I can!"
The flame-red peony opens
its thick wide petals spread
a child's head like a hard bud in the center.
It is circled by a burning crown
studded with fire
glorious at delivery.

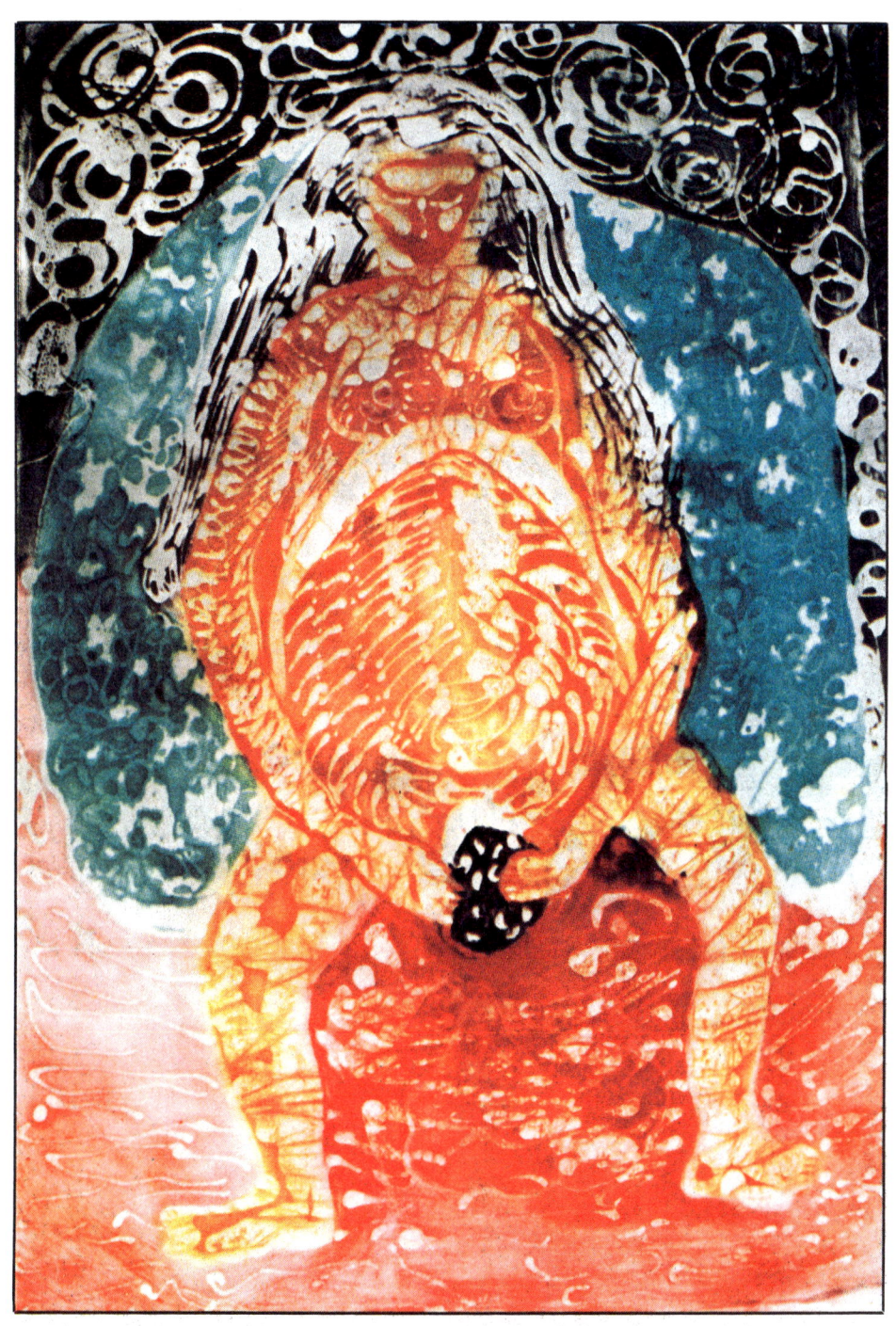

Birthing

Under the arch of bone
dips a child
pauses
lifts, slides forward
wet and honey-smooth.

Launched into life
from womb harbor into swirling sea
and then to find afresh
a safe haven in her cradling hands.

Womb power

Birth is power.
Not frail and fancy suffering
not a passive waiting on life
not polite obedience to medical commands or coaxing.

The clouds burst.
Woman arches over all
queen of night, goddess of creation
in splendor and strength of majesty.

The tempest of life's beginning
sweeps through her body.
The flower opens.
Thick petals part.
The hard bud pushes down
and spreads wide
tissues that burn with sacred fire.

Calm after storm

After the soaring, a peace
like swans settling on the lake.
After the tumult and the roaring winds
silence.
After daring to leap over the chasm
feet know the certainty of good earth.
The tide swept in through every crevice of her body
and now she is beached and safe.
She looks down to see a child
amazed.

Welcoming

Reach down
hands feel the firm, warm curve
of the baby's head.
This storm of feeling
the great, grinding mill of labor
has brought me to this sweet welcoming.
I greet my child first by touch
sensing through quick, eager fingers as blind read Braille
only then
to see, hear, breathe deep.

Welcome, little one.

Birth fulfilled

The child comes to the breast
latches on, suckles deep
tugs at my essence.

Womb tightens, grasps firm
presses down
and the placenta slides out
soft, sensuous pleasure.

The greeting

You are mine and I am yours.
Nothing else matters.
The earth could crack—
but I have known
this moment.
Cradled in light
sprouting a million wings
festooned in stars
like a candle piercing the darkness
a woman holds her child.